Greater Tha
Se
Reviews from Readers

I think the series is wonderful and beneficial for tourists to get information before visiting the city.

-Seckin Zumbul, Izmir Turkey

I am a world traveler who has read many trip guides but this one really made a difference for me. I would call it a heartfelt creation of a local guide expert instead of just a guide.

-Susy, Isla Holbox, Mexico

New to the area like me, this is a must have!

-Joe, Bloomington, USA

This is a good series that gets down to it when looking for things to do at your destination without having to read a novel for just a few ideas.

-Rachel, Monterey, USA

Good information to have to plan my trip to this destination.

-Pennie Farrell, Mexico

Great ideas for a port day.

-Mary Martin USA

Aptly titled, you won't just be a tourist after reading this book. You'll be greater than a tourist!

-Alan Warner, Grand Rapids, USA

Even though I only have three days to spend in San Miguel in an upcoming visit, I will use the author's suggestions to guide some of my time there. An easy read - with chapters named to guide me in directions I want to go.

 -Robert Catapano, USA

Great insights from a local perspective! Useful information and a very good value!

 -Sarah, USA

This series provides an in-depth experience through the eyes of a local. Reading these series will help you to travel the city in with confidence and it'll make your journey a unique one.

-Andrew Teoh, Ipoh, Malaysia

GREATER THAN A TOURIST- LISBON PORTUGAL

50 Travel Tips from a Local

Carolyn Campbell

Cover designed by: Ivana Stamenkovic
Cover Image: https://pixabay.com/photos/lisbon-portugal-alfama-building-344765/

CZYK Publishing Since 2011.

Greater Than a Tourist

Lock Haven, PA

ISBN: 9781692761219

>TOURIST

50 TRAVEL TIPS FROM A LOCAL

BOOK DESCRIPTION

Are you excited about planning your next trip? Do you want to try something new? Would you like some guidance from a local? If you answered yes to any of these questions, then this Greater Than a Tourist book is for you. *Greater Than a Tourist-Lisbon, Portugal* by Carolyn Campbell offers the inside scoop on Lisbon, Portugal. Most travel books tell you how to travel like a tourist. Although there is nothing wrong with that, as part of the Greater Than a Tourist series, this book will give you travel tips from someone who has lived at your next travel destination.

In these pages, you will discover advice that will help you throughout your stay. This book will not tell you exact addresses or store hours but instead will give you excitement and knowledge from a local that you may not find in other smaller print travel books.

Travel like a local. Slow down, stay in one place, and get to know the people and culture. By the time you finish this book, you will be eager and prepared to travel to your next destination.

Inside this travel guide book you will find:

- Insider tips from a local.

- Packing and planning list.

- List of travel questions to ask yourself or others while traveling.

- A place to write your travel bucket list.

OUR STORY

Traveling is a passion of the Greater than a Tourist book series creator. Lisa studied abroad in college, and for their honeymoon Lisa and her husband toured Europe. During her travels to Malta, an older man tried to give her some advice based on his own experience living on the island since he was a young boy. She was not sure if she should talk to the stranger but was interested in his advice. When traveling to some places she was wary to talk to locals because she was afraid that they weren't being genuine. Through her travels, Lisa learned how much locals had to share with tourists. Lisa created the Greater Than a Tourist book series to help connect people with locals. A topic that locals are very passionate about sharing.

TABLE OF CONTENTS

BOOK DESCRIPTION

OUR STORY

TABLE OF CONTENTS

DEDICATION

ABOUT THE AUTHOR

HOW TO USE THIS BOOK

FROM THE PUBLISHER

WELCOME TO

> TOURIST

1. Learn a Few Words of Portuguese

2. Try to Understand a Little of the History of Portugal

3. Getting Around in Lisbon

4. Enjoy a Salgado

5. Where to get the Best Ice Cream

6. Find the Statue Who Lost His Head

7. Try Out an Electric Scooter

8. Why is There a Rhino?

9. The Best Pastries in Lisbon

10. Chill out in the Park

11. Go For a Run

12. What Do a King of England and a Queen of Fado Have In Common?

13. Picnic in The Sun in the Jardim da Estrella

14. Jamor Urban Park

15. Hike Monsanto

16. Parque das Pedras

17. Sardines - Grilled or Ceramic

18. Cocktails by the River

19. When to Visit

20. Visit the Águas Livres Aqueduct

21. Museo do Combatente

22. Sao Jorge Castle and Martim Moniz

23. Spectacular Views

24. Find the Lisbon Assassinations Plaque

25. Listen to Fado

26. Ajuda National Palace

27. Travelling with Children

28. Best Beaches to Surf

29. Football Legends

30. Spice and Sailors

31. LX Factory and Ler Devagar

32. Tram 28: A Visitor Favourite

33. Time Out Market

34. Bordalo Segundo Garbage Street Art

35. Stop for a Drink

36. Bacalhau

37. Try Traditional Sour Cherry Liqueur

38. Vhils Street Art

39. Train Along the Linha

40. Cascais Old Town and Museum District

41. Marechal Carmona Park

42. Museu Condes de Castro Guimaraes

43. Bike Along the Red Path to Guincho Beach

44. Boca do Inferno

45. Cascais Beaches

46. Sintra UNESCO World Heritage Site

47. Traditional Sintra Treats

48. Sintra

49. Tram Trip to Apple Beach

50. Not Just a Summer Destination

TOP REASONS TO BOOK THIS TRIP

Packing and Planning Tips

Travel Questions

Travel Bucket List

NOTES

DEDICATION

This book is dedicated to Jamie, Alec, Hugh and Xanthe for being so much fun and always willing to try anything, and to my parents, Mary and John Summers for fostering my love of both travel, and words.

ABOUT THE AUTHOR

Carolyn Campbell is a freelance travel writer, military wife and mother of 3. Seasoned world traveller and current expat, Carolyn loves sharing insider tips on the destinations she visits. She enjoys searching out local culinary specialties but draws the line at eating insects. Brought to Lisbon by her husband's job she continues to immerse herself in the language and culture of Portugal.

HOW TO USE THIS BOOK

The *Greater Than a Tourist* book series was written by someone who has lived in an area for over three months. The goal of this book is to help travelers either dream or experience different locations by providing opinions from a local. The author has made suggestions based on their own experiences. Please check before traveling to the area in case the suggested places are unavailable.

Travel Advisories: As a first step in planning any trip abroad, check the Travel Advisories for your intended destination.
https://travel.state.gov/content/travel/en/traveladvisories/traveladvisories.html

FROM THE PUBLISHER

Traveling can be one of the most important parts of a person's life. The anticipation and memories that you have are some of the best. As a publisher of the Greater Than a Tourist, as well as the popular *50 Things to Know* book series, we strive to help you learn about new places, spark your imagination, and inspire you. Wherever you are and whatever you do I wish you safe, fun, and inspiring travel.

Lisa Rusczyk Ed. D.
CZYK Publishing

WELCOME TO
> TOURIST

"We leave something of ourselves behind when we leave a place, we stay there, even though we go away. And there are things in us that we can find again only by going back there."

— Pascal Mercier, Night Train to Lisbon

An imposing statue of Cristo Rei himself stands guard over Lisbon and certainly enjoys an enviable view of this beautiful city. From the Tejo river up to the seven hills that shelter the historic city, there are treasures to discover at every turn. Whether you're here for the castles and monuments to Portugal's past as a seafaring superpower, or to kick back and enjoy the surf by day and the hip bars and restaurants by night, you won't fail to find your happy place here.

Lisbon
Portugal

Lisbon
Climate

	High	Low
January	59	47
February	61	48
March	65	51
April	68	53
May	72	57
June	78	61
July	82	64
August	83	65
September	80	63
October	73	59
November	64	53
December	59	49

GreaterThanaTourist.com

Temperatures are in Fahrenheit degrees.
Source: NOAA

1. LEARN A FEW WORDS OF PORTUGUESE

Although Portugal, and Lisbon, in particular, has a very high proportion of people who speak excellent English, it's easy to learn just a few words of Portuguese. Portuguese people are very polite, and pleasantries are always observed, it is customary to say 'bom dia' (good morning) or 'boa tarde' (good afternoon) when entering a shop, or to the cashier serving you in the supermarket and polite to also say thank you, obrigado (for a man) or obrigada (for a woman) and bom dia / boa tarde as you leave a shop or cafe.

People appreciate that you have made a small effort with their language and generally if they see that you have exhausted your Portuguese they will switch to English to help you out.

2. TRY TO UNDERSTAND A LITTLE OF THE HISTORY OF PORTUGAL

A public toilet isn't necessarily where you would go to look for amazing artworks or an insight into the history of a city but secreted in a little alleyway in Alfama you'll find both.

Muralist Nuno Saraiva painted his history of Lisbon from the founding of the town by the Phonecians right through the Portuguese Inquisition, and shows in cartoons the earthquake of 1755, up to the Carnation Revolution in 1974 in colourful, easy to digest comic strip form.

3. GETTING AROUND IN LISBON

Driving in Lisbon is not for the faint-hearted! The streets in the older part of town are narrow and often cobbled with typical calcada Portuguesa and cobwebbed with tram tracks and one way systems so in all honesty, it is easier and less stressful to catch a cab or use public transport.

The Viva Viagem card is the easiest way to pay for all public transport trips in the city; it can be used on the train, bus, metro, ferry and even the funicular railway. You can buy your Viva Viagem card at any ticket office in a metro, ferry of a train station or you can use the automated ticket machines, and each person must have their own card, although under 4s travel free with a paying parent. The card itself will cost around 50 cents then you can charge it in one of three ways

● A single ticket to pay for a specific journey valid for one hour 1.50

● A 24-hour ticket which is activated by the first journey and which come with various options for travel zones

● The Zapping option allows you to simply put credit on the car to be used as you need it

Uber is popular in the city, and many people use the app for both long and short journeys, and licensed taxis are plentiful and available via app, phone or at taxi ranks.

4. ENJOY A SALGADO

Cafe culture is a way of life in Lisbon and snacking is a great way to discover some of the excellent little cafes, snack bars and bakeries the city has to offer. Salgados are savory finger food snacks that are enjoyed from late morning onwards but are at their most delicious when fresh out of the over at around 11 am; locals often enjoy a salgado and a lambreta (a tiny 150ml glass of ice-cold beer) standing at a cafe counter.

Salgados are usually fried and should be eaten warm, avoid anything that looks as if it has been in a display case feeling sad all morning and find somewhere that cooks fresh batches often. The pastel de bacalhau is without a doubt the most popular and is a delicious little morsel made from flaked salt cod, potato, eggs and parsley quenelled and deep-fried. Rissois de camarao, the breaded half-moon pastries filled with shrimp and bechamel sauce are also very popular, along with puff pastries called chamucas or croquettes filled with any combination of cheese, ham, or spinach. Empandas are also worth trying;

these snacks are small pies rather than being a fried delicacy and are usually filled with chicken or duck

5. WHERE TO GET THE BEST ICE CREAM

Nanarella, Davvero, or Santini? These three gelaterias in Lisbon always provoke discussion on which is the best. In the name of research, I have tried various flavours from all three a few times. Whether you're exploring in the Alfama or enjoying beach life in Cascais you are never far from top-quality gelato. Nanarella is near the Palacete de São Bento and is open late into the evening so you can enjoy a treat after dinner. Davvero's central location is near the Mercado da Ribeira, close enough to to the Tejo to stroll along the riverbank with your ice cream cone and there is an additional shop in the Centro Cultural de Belem to the west of the city. All three ice cream parlours have a range of delicious flavours from mango to maribunta (choc chip) but Santini's edges it for me, there is a branch in the Time Out Market as well as the two original shops in Cascais, and the choices change often enough to keep it interesting.

19

My top tip is the raspberry sorbet, and you can even buy a litre in a stay-cold container to take home.

6. FIND THE STATUE WHO LOST HIS HEAD

In the centre of Rossio Square stands a statue of King Pedro VI atop a tall column. The figure of Pedro VI is cast in bronze and shows him in his general's uniform and royal cloak with a crown of laurel atop his head and a representation of the Constitutional Charter of 1826 in his right hand. Ranged around the base of the corinthian column are the allegorical figures of Wisdom, Strength, Justice, and Moderation, the qualities attributed to the 4th king of Portugal and 1st Emperor of Brazil.

Local legend has it that the statue itself was initially designed for Emperor Maximillian I of Mexico and was on its way to the New World on a ship via Lisbon when the news came in 1867 that he had been shot. According to the stories the statue was offloaded into a Lisbon warehouse where it languished until someone had the bright idea to repurpose it for Rossio square People say that Maximillian's head was struck off and a replacement likeness of King Pedro IV was cast and attached in time for the statue to be erected in 1870 and this is the reason that the column is so tall.

Local historians have since proved this story fake by pointing out the details that clearly mark the statues as representing a portugues figure, such as the Portugues Coat of Arms on the buttons and the Portuguese Order of the Tower and Sword collar. It's still a fun story and one which you are likely to hear tour guides tell their groups in Rossio Square.

7. TRY OUT AN ELECTRIC SCOOTER

The new thing in Lisbon is the electric scooter, and they are super popular with locals and visitors alike. The scooters (trotinettes in Portuguese) are easy to unlock with a app downloaded on your phone, and there are often reps near the main scooter parks who will give you a discount code to hit the open road. Be very careful where you ride and park up though, although you can rent a scooter on the river walk near the Time Out Market to scoot on up to the city centre Praça de Comercio, you cannot park in the city and will incur a fine if you do.

8. WHY IS THERE A RHINO?

When you're in Lisbon, you have to visit Belem Tower. Out to the west of the city where the River Tejo meets the Atlantic ocean, you'll be wowed by this 16th-century masterpiece. A famous Lisbon landmark this mini-castle is the point from which the explorers set sail for the new world. See if you can find the rhino sculpted on the outer wall of the tower!

In 1514 Don Alfonso de Albuquerque, Governor of Portuguese India wanted to build a fortress in Diu, which was governed by Sultan Muzafar. He sent an envoy to the Sultan asking permission and giving a generous amount of gift to smooth the process along, the request was refused, but the Sultan sent him a rhino as a token of his regard. The rhino was subsequently loaded onto a ship to Lisbon as a present for King Manuel I. The whole of Europe was fascinated by this bizarre creature when it arrived in Portugal, and it made its home in the Royal Ribeira Palace until it was sent as part of envoy to Rome to the Pope. Unfortunately the ship carrying the rhino was caught in a storm and sank off the coast of Genoa.

A figure of the rhinoceros now decorates one of the bartizans of the Torre de Belem.

9. THE BEST PASTRIES IN LISBON

The pastel de nata or custard tart is best eaten with a coffee for a quick jolt of energy. It was originally made in the Sao Jeronimo monastery close by and the original recipe is still a secret. You can eat the original, and the best custard tart at the Pasteis de Belem bakery but the queue of tourists often snakes out of the door.

What those in the know do to get their sugar fix do is stroll past the hordes and wind their way past the kitchen, to the back of the bakery. When you see a little patio, take a seat, and a waiter in a white apron will be happy to bring you a coffee and a pastel de nata to enjoy at your leisure.

You will be revitalised by your snack and back out, enjoying the sights before the back of the outside queue has even been served.

10. CHILL OUT IN THE PARK

Located in Monsanto country park known as the lungs of Lisbon this park is brilliant for all ages. Parque do Alvito is great fun and fenced all around so if your child is a runner you can be sure they can't escape into the carpark without being noticed by the docent on the gate.

As you walk through the park, you will come across three separate levels with a playground on each, connected by both stairs and a ramp for prams or wheelchairs. All of the playground equipment is clean and modern and is on a base of bouncy rubber tiles to protect little hands and knees.

The first playground you come to is suitable for ages 1-12, it has swings with baskets and low-level equipment so even the smallest children can play happily. As you stroll up the path you will find the next playground, suitable for ages 3-12, connected to the lower level by steps and slides, this part has even more play equipment, including rocking animals to ride. The upper-level playground is for 4-12-year-olds and features an awesome pirate ship and tents to play hide and seek in.

There are plenty of picnic tables dotted around the park so you can bring a snack to fuel the fun, and there is a cafe located near the pond so you can grab a drink. There is also access to clean toilet facilities and a baby change area.

11. GO FOR A RUN

Lisbon's maze of cobbled streets and heavy traffic isn't ideal for running, having to stop at intersections and dodge pedestrians doesn't make for a relaxing way to stretch your legs. There are some much better routes to tackle whatever your level of running expertise.

- Run from the Praça de Comércio along the river path to Belém and enjoy river breezes
- Run on the boardwalk at Parque das Nações, stretching from the Vasco da Gama bridge to the Oceanarium this is a safe running space
- Run the circumference of the Paraue Eduardo VII and enjoy the city centre green space

12. WHAT DO A KING OF ENGLAND AND A QUEEN OF FADO HAVE IN COMMON?

They both have a gorgeous park just metres away from one another in central Lisbon. Parque Edward VII is the larger or the two parks and was named to honour the British monarch in advance of his visit to Lisbon in 1903.

The main attraction of this park for the adults in the family are the amazing views across beautifully landscaped gardens down to the river Tejo. The garden slopes from the river up towards the centre of the city, and there are three greenhouses with a variety of native and exotic plants to explore. The Estufa Fria unheated greenhouse is the most popular place to visit, followed by the Estufa Quente hothouse filled with tropical plants, then the Estufa Doce which houses the succulent plants.

If your kids love thrills check out the zipline in the playground next to the Estufa Fria, there are also swings, slides, and a climbing area if you like your fun more gentle. Just in front of this greenhouse is where you'll find the lake filled with fish and with ducks paddling serenely along. If you feel like a stroll, take a walk up the typical Portuguese mosaic pavements bordering the maze of geometric hedging, up to the observation tower. There are several cafes in the park which have clean toilet facilities, including a pizza kiosk.

Jardim Amalia Rodrigues, next door named for the celebrated fado singer links Parque Edward VII to Monsanto country park.

13. PICNIC IN THE SUN IN THE JARDIM DA ESTRELLA

✗

This is a favourite with locals, and whatever time of day you go you'll be sharing the space with picnicking families, retired gentlemen chatting in the shade and children playing with a ball on the lush grass.

The playground is well kept and a fabulous place for children to stretch out their muscles and get some fresh air. The play area is fenced off and has a fun climbing frame which sports a lion's head, a slide, and several swings.

The park is pleasant to wander in, and pushchair and wheelchair friendly, the paths meander around tropical planting on various levels. You will eventually find the parks' bandstand and in the summer will often be treated to performances by local musicians.

Head to the lake to sit on a bench in the shade to watch the swans glide by and have a drink in the late afternoon while the younger members of the party play hide and seek amongst the trees.

14. JAMOR URBAN PARK

Next to the Nation Stadium, which was built in 1939 and revamped in 2014, is the urban park of Jamor was conceived as a community sports facility open to everyone.

From bike paths to a path especially created for spotting some of the 70+ species of bird that make their home in the park, there is something for everyone. Space is well cared for with plenty of room for picnicking or going for a run along one of the looping trails that border the canals.

If you are feeling particularly adventurous, you could try Adventure Park (fee payable) which has a series of treetop trails to try out, which include tightrope walks, hanging tunnels and slides. If you prefer something a little closer to the ground there is a mini-golf course of 18 holes, you can borrow the clubs and balls for free, but there are limited numbers.

You can rent a canoe and relax on the river, then recharge with a picnic at one of the picturesque spots furnished with wooden benches.

If you are missing the gym, there is a series of 12 fitness stations in a circuit so you can enjoy the fresh air and enjoy this beautiful park. If you fancy a game of football, badminton or volleyball, you can enjoy the well kept open green areas or use one of the purpose-built synthetic courts.

15. HIKE MONSANTO

The 1000 hectares that make up the forest park of Monsanto is great fun to explore. In the park, there are various multi-sports arenas, an amphitheatre, mini-golf and tennis courts and even a fantastic campsite with a swimming pool.

The best way to get from the centre of Lisbon to Monsanto park is to take a walk along the pedestrianised / cycle path the Coredo Verde from Parque Eduardo VII, through the Amalia Rodrigues Garden. This beautiful route will take you to

Monsanto park in around an hour on foot, and the route is clearly marked and easy to walk.

The Espaco Monsanto Interpretation Centre is the best place to start, check out the small exhibition on the park, and from there you can pick up a map or guidebook and decide which activities you like the look of.

Alameda Keil do Amaral is a 10-hectare area in the south of Monsanto Forest Park, there is a small amphitheater with a spectacular view over the Tejo and the southern outskirts of the city. You can stroll or cycle along the many paths of the Mata de Sao Domingos de Benfica which is a vast area with a range of natural habitats often used for environmental education workshops. This area has a circuit of fitness equipment in a shady spot, picnic areas, and a children's play area.

16. PARQUE DAS PEDRAS

Parque das Pedras is a reasonably new addition to the list of open-air activities in Lisbon and is a great place to challenge yourself; you could have a go on the 12m climbing wall, or try a climb in the bouldering area or treetop trail. There is plenty to keep the children occupied in Monsanto too, Alto da Serafina Park has a fantastic play area and cafe, Calhau park has lots of space to run around, and the Moinhos de Santana Urban Park and Quinta da Fonte have children's' play equipment and room to play sports, run or cycle.

17. SARDINES – GRILLED OR CERAMIC

The Portuguese only eat sardines that are a maximum of 24 hours from swimming around the deep blue sea, and most importantly of all only eat them in months which have no 'r,' namely May, June, July, and August. You have to eat them grilled fresh and well salted, and they taste best when you eat them outdoors by the sea on a sunny day. In season you'll see handwritten signs outside bars and restaurants letting you know há sardinhas, there are fresh sardines on the menu.

You can buy cute souvenir sardines all year round, the ceramic ones are beautiful and painted with all sorts of modern and traditional motifs and patterns and make a great souvenir by which to remember your trip. Celebrated Portuguese artist and ceramicist Rafael Bordallo Pinheiro (1846-1905) opened his ceramic factory in Caldas de Raina to the north of Lisbon in 1884. His original concept was to focus on the style and natural motifs of Portugal in the form of tin-glazed pottery and this continues today. The bigger pieces such as bowls and jugs often take the form of leaves of flowers and the ceramic sardine collection changes often to stay apace with popular culture.

18. COCKTAILS BY THE RIVER

Park is an amazing rooftop bar is situated on top of a multi-story car park in the historic Bairro Alto is popular for sundowners on warm summer evenings. This hip bar features in a lot of Instagram stories as the view over Lisbon is second to none. There are a wide variety of cocktails on offer from the trusted

33

classics to funky new concoctions. Try The snacks and light meals which are available in the early evening to help give you stamina for the dancing later on! Once you have climbed past all the cars right up to the 6th floor where the bar is you can relax to the sounds of soul and funk played by the resident DJ. Kick back amongst the tropical plants and look across the Tejo river to the 25 de Abril bridge and the Christ Redeemer statue.

Topo is another Lisbon hidden gem, a rooftop bar situated on the top floor of an old shopping mall in the Martim Moniz area. The entrance is a tucked away, but it is definitely worth the effort. It has spectacular views over the Castelo Sao Jorge and the rooftops of downtown Lisbon.

If you can't bear to tear yourself away from the river bank, then you might fancy pausing for an aperitif at Pitcher Cocktails an old fashioned tricycle-cum-cocktail bar. You can order delicious cocktails such as the mojito or caipiroska or go for a refreshing alcohol-free passion fruit lemonade to enjoy on the esplanade next to the Tejo.

19. WHEN TO VISIT

Lisbon is just as much fun in the cooler months as in the summer; it's quieter and more comfortable to do the 'must-do' sights without tripping over tourists. Alright, you probably won't be enjoying the surf vibe that summer brings, but the relative tranquility is just as rewarding.

Lisbon seems to have hit everyone's top city break list, and for the last couple of summers, it has been difficult to experience the main attractions of the city without either getting up a dawn (and who wants to do that on holiday?) or being surrounded by other eager travellers. The best time to come to get a flavour of local's Lisbon is when the holiday season winds down in the autumn and winter.

20. VISIT THE ÁGUAS LIVRES AQUEDUCT

The Águas Livres Aqueduct is perfect for those seeking an alternative glimpse into a historic site with different perspective over Lisbon. A stroll along the road over the aqueduct is an experience which shouldn't be missed. In the past a lack of safe drinking water was a considerable concern for the city of Lisbon, the water of the Tejo estuary was far too salty to process, so the idea was born to take advantage of water from the Carenque river alley, in the Belas region.

The most extensive public works project ever built in Portugal, with a length of 58 km, the construction of the Águas Livres Aqueduct was funded by a tax known as "Real de Água" which was applied to goods such as olive oil, wine, and meat. An idiosyncrasy of the aqueduct's architecture is that it incorporates two distinct styles: up to the city border, the structure is purely utilitarian when the aqueduct enters the city the structure of the aqueduct becomes more ornate and Baroque. It covers an area of 941 meters, is composed of a total of 35 arches, including the largest stone arch in the world, reaching 65.29 meters in height and 28.86 meters in width.

21. MUSEO DO COMBATENTE

X

This is run by the Portuguese Veterans Association and is housed in an old military fort at the mouth of the Tejo river near the Torre de Belem. This museum has a series of displays which detail Portugal's military campaigns from the First World War to the Colonial Wars in Angola and Mozambique of the 1970s.

The exhibits tell the story of a variety of regiments in the conflicts over the years and are home to period tanks and artillery. The museum in the Fort of Bom Sucesso is dedicated to the fallen from all the disputes that Portugal has been involved in and two soldiers guard the memorial chapel and perpetual flame outside the museum.

22. SAO JORGE CASTLE AND MARTIM MONIZ

Have you heard the legend of Martin Moniz? He was the soldier who ended the 4-month siege of Sao Jorge castle in 1147 and who has gone down in

37

history because of his altruism. The story goes that the knight Martim Moniz discovered a side gate of the castle open at a time when the moors had decamped inside the walls to protect themselves from the Christians who wanted to reconquer Lisbon. The small gate was open, and Martim alerted his comrades who raced around to gain access to the castle, the Moorish guards noticed that the Christian knights were trying to enter but as they closed the gate, the brave Martim wedged his body in the gap, thus holding it open. He was crushed to death, but his name has been legend ever since. The famous Martim Moniz gate is to the north of the castle and overlooks a square which also bears his name.

After your visit to the castle head over to Miradouro Santa Luzia. An excellent place from which to look out over the city, this beautiful viewpoint has a rose garden to wander around, spectacular views over the city to the Tejo beyond. Check out the tile mural of Martim Moniz at the gates of the Castelo Sao Jorge tucked away in the corner

23. SPECTACULAR VIEWS

Panoramic de Monsanto is an off the beaten track place from which to get a fantastic view of the city. The old abandoned restaurant doesn't look much from its graffiti daubed exterior, but the views from the upper floor are second to none. Walk up through the pine trees to find the building and go carefully up the steps until you find the panoramic window with the tiled guide to the landmarks of the city on the cill with views stretching from the 25th of April Bridge to the Benfica Stadium. Head over to the other side of the building to enjoys views right up to Sintra and over the Atlantic.

24. FIND THE LISBON ASSASSINATIONS PLAQUE

The Age of Discoveries made Portugal rich, but by 1890 those riches were all but gone, and the country was on its knees financially. King Carlos 1 was on the throne and in the first crisis of his reign had to cede land in Africa to the British to avoid war. This cost him the goodwill of the Portuguese people, and by

39

1906 the government was collapsing, and society was in chaos, Prime Minister Joao Franco was ruling by decree and democracy was crumbling fast. Many citizens felt angry that they were effectively living under a dictatorship, and political temperatures were running high.

King Carlos 1 returned to Lisbon in 1908 with his family from the Alentejo, riding in an open carriage across the main square in Lisbon. Terreiro do Paço, decimated in the earthquake of 1755 had been restored to a bustling market square, and the King, Crown Prince and the rest of the family were keen to be visible to the people of Lisbon. As the carriage crossed the square shots rang out from the crowd, two bullets hit King Carlos 1 killing him immediately. Crown Prince Luis Felipe stood up, drawing his revolver when a second assassin jumped up onto the carriage steps and shot him in the head, fatally wounding him. The killers were quickly apprehended and killed on the scene by the police, and the royal carriage made haste to the Naval Arsenal nearby.

Prince Manuel, the younger son of the King, recovered from his wounds and was made king a mere 20 minutes after the death of his father and brother, but his reign was short ending in August 1910 when the first elections were held in Portugal. The bodies of King Carlos 1 and Prince Luis Felipe lay in state in the National Pantheon in Lisbon where many other prominent figures of Portugal's past now also lie.

The plaque commemorating the assassinations is at the Corner of Rua do Arsenal and Praça do Comércio

25. LISTEN TO FADO

Fado originated from the port districts of Lisbon, Alfama, Mouraria and the Bairro Alto, in early 19th century in Lisbon. Performers were generally from urban working-class such as sailors, prostitutes and dockworkers who not only sang but also danced and beat time to the fado guitar.

In the latter half of the 19th century, the performers became singers alone and were depicted as rough hoarse-voiced singers using slang and playing with a flick knife. If you're interested in knowing more about Fado, then the Fado Museum in Alfama is excellent.

Tasca do Chico is an excellent place to listen to fado informally, you may be treated to fado by celebrities singers such as Mariza, but more often you get the authentic fado vadio (literally translated as a vagabond, but which means "amateur" in the language of fado). As a general rule, you shouldn't talk while the artists are performing. The place is tiny and very popular, so it's wise to book ahead for fado which starts at 9 pm.

26. AJUDA NATIONAL PALACE

The Ajuda National Palace is a must-see in Lisbon, if you're interested in the splendour and ostentation of the last years of the Portuguese Royal family. Construction on the top of the Ajuda hill, with a superb view of the Tejo River, began in 1796, of the palace that was to finally replace the wooden building that housed the king in the years following the earthquake of 1755

The palace was conceived as one of the largest palaces in Europe, complete with rolling grounds but that plan did not come to fruition as the royal family decamped to Brazil in 1807 following the Napoleonic Wars. Although the Ajuda National Palace is essentially an unfinished project, the Ajuda National Palace is still grand enough to deserve a visit to see how the royal family's daily affairs unfolded.

On the ornately decorated ground floor, you'll find the royal family's private rooms, including the dining room, the Blue Room, a richly decorated sitting room, and the Queen D. Maria Pia's rooms, with its collection of fine porcelain, and the stunning Winter Garden. This floor is a brief glimpse into what was important to the 19th century bourgeois in their private homes.

The Noble Floor was intended for gala receptions and was the public face of the royal family. The Grand Dining Room is still the location of presidential banquets today, and you can admire the 18th-century Chinese porcelain service. The highlights of the Throne Room are the Portuguese-made thrones themselves, although the decor of the whole room is breathtaking.

In 1910, with the Founding of the Republic and the exile of the royal family, the palace was mothballed to later reopen in 1968 as a museum with the most extensive collection of Portuguese art in the world.

27. TRAVELLING WITH CHILDREN

Portugal, in general, is a fabulous place to travel with children, they are welcomed in restaurants and cafes, and people will often chat with them or tell you how beautiful your little angels are. Lisbon is a particularly great place to bring children as the city is so compact it's easy to walk around and there are cafes and gelaterias at every turn to give tiny legs a rest and refresh. There are a host of play parks and child-friendly activities including tuk-tuk rides or a trip to the zoo.

If you're here in the summer do bear in mind that the city can often reach in excess of 30c and it is still humid at night so you will probably need to build lots of breaks into your itinerary and take advantage of the beaches just outside Lisbon to cool off.

28. BEST BEACHES TO SURF

Lisbon has excellent waves right on its doorstep all year round, so it's the perfect holiday if you fancy a mix of surf and culture. Carcavelos beach is an easy drive or train journey from Lisbon and is popular for its consistently good waves all year round. It is suitable for all levels and has a variety of surf schools available for lessons or equipment hire.

The Costa da Caparica is south of Lisbon across the river, this stretch gets surf and swell year-round due to its exposed location and is especially fun as it has rights and lefts that beak at different stages all along the beach.

Praia da Poca is west of Lisbon and as a reef break which is better for intermediate to advanced surfers. Also to the west is Praia do Guincho which is not only a beautiful 1km stretch of golden sand but one of the best beach breaks in the area. The waves are usually mellow in the summer, but it can get big and bold at other times of the year.

29. FOOTBALL LEGENDS

Benfica stadium, properly called Estádio da Luz is a city landmark. If you visit Lisbon when Benfica are playing at home it's well worth queueing for a ticket and enjoying the spectacle and atmosphere of a match.

The club has a museum and offers a tour around the stadium if you're keen to see inside the distinctive building. The museum is easy to access in the well-signposted grounds of the stadium and is opposite the club shop. You will have the opportunity to see the silverware that Benfica has won, which includes two European Cups as well as a host of national awards.

There is also a section on the club's history and notable players of the past including Eusebio, whose body can be found in the Pantheon in central Lisbon. I particularly enjoyed the chart that catalogues the club's achievements alongside a chart detailing important events in world history so that you have a historical context.

Don't forget to visit the brief display on the eagles that are the Benfica mascot, in fact, and the club still stages a flyby around the stadium by one of the resident live eagles before home games. The tour of the stadium, which includes the director's box, away dressing room, tunnel, and pitch is conducted via an app which gives you information and anecdotes at various points.

Sporting Lisbon the great rivals of Benfica play at the Estádio de Alvalide which also offers a tour. The tour is similar in style, and you can enjoy seeing the dressing rooms and going onto the pitchside. A member of staff conducts this tour, and the human touch enhances the experience as the guide can usually tell you a story or two from their own experience. The museum is enjoyable if slightly smaller than Benfica's, but the section devoted to local heroes Luis Figo and Ronaldo is worth your time.

30. SPICE AND SAILORS

The Jeronimos Monastery in Belem is accessible via tram, bus or metro; hop off right outside the monastery. The vast building overlooks the wide Tejo river flowing out to the ocean and in the Age of Discoveries the church previously on the site, was the final place for sailors to pray before they set out for the New World. Portuguese hero Vasco da Gama prayed here with his crew before their successful trip toward Asia in 1497, and this prompted the building of the current monastery in starting in 1501 and finishing 100 years later in 1601.

The monastery and attached church are well worth visiting, if you go inside you are still able to walk around the two-story cloisters and admire the breathtaking architectural details inspired by the monastery's position next to the water and the marvels brought back from far off lands. You have to buy your tickets in the main booth then walk around to the entrance, in the summertime, there are huge hot queues for both in full sun which does not make for a peaceful, contemplative experience. Go in the winter, and you're likely to have the place to yourself.

31. LX FACTORY AND LER DEVAGAR

This old industrial complex dating from 1846 was reborn in 2008 as a cool art and cafe space. The factory-style architecture was maintained as a complex of exhibition spaces initially, and shops, restaurants, and cafes were later added. The bookshop Ler Devagar in a former print shop is one of the highlights of the LX Factory complex, it maintains the old printing press on display, and the bicycle artwork by Pietro Proserpina hanging over patrons heads is a fun touch.

Don't forget to sample some of the treats available here; the LX Cheesecake Factory is an institution and the chocolate cake which is the specialty of cafe Landau has been named by Time Out as the best in the city.

32. TRAM 28: A VISITOR FAVOURITE

A favourite symbol of Lisbon is its iconic yellow trams or electricos as they're known in Portuguese, they are all over the city and are great fun to ride. The classic rollercoaster-esque ride up and down the hills of the city is the number 28 tram but in the summer? Forget it. Too crowded, queues at tram stops a mile long, no seats, can't see out of the windows, risk of pickpockets, it all just saps the fun out of the experience.

The winter is an entirely different proposition, go on a weekday from November to February, and you will have a great ride. My top tip is to get the metro or walk, depending on where you're staying and how fit you're feeling, up to the top of the line at Campo de Ourique and head right down into the city towards the Martim Moniz stop. Most visitors get on at Martim Moniz as it's closer to the historic centre so if you do the reverse you're almost guaranteed to have the pick of the seats and a fantastic view.

33. TIME OUT MARKET

This busy covered market is a favourite dining spot for locals and visitors alike. More than 40 kiosks bring all the varied flavours of Lisbon together under one roof.

Amazing juicy burgers made with Portuguese beef, top quality sushi, traditional salted cod dishes, and mouth-watering pastries jostle for space on the vast communal tables in the centre of the market.

Everything in the Time Out Market has been selected, sampled and enjoyed by an independent panel of the city's foodie experts from Time Out magazine.

There are over 40 restaurants, a cooking academy where you can learn how to make Portuguese and international specialties, a bar, a club and a shop selling local artisan-made gifts.

Try a little bit of everything! Then stop for a drink at the bar and have a look at what's going on in the open kitchen-classroom.

34. BORDALO SEGUNDO GARBAGE STREET ART

Lisbon is a city with fantastic street art and fabulous paintings are all over buildings and walls wherever you go.

Street artist Bordallo II makes amazing sculptures using rubbish found dumped or encountered in abandoned factories. The idea behind the series is to raise the issue of the volume of waste produced by society and create awareness of the fact that our throwaway culture has created a severe problem for the environment.

If you search a little and keep your eyes open as you wander the city, you will see a few of his pieces around Lisbon. The raccoon can be seen from the garden of the Museu Berardo in Belém, and at the LX Factory, you can see the wasp. The artist has a Facebook page to which he posts his new creations locations

35. STOP FOR A DRINK

As well as great food, Lisbon has a wealth of drink options, both alcoholic and soft. Beer served tends to be one of two national brands, Sagres or Superbock and is served as a caneca (300cl) or an imperial (500cl).

Wine sold is usually from Portuguese vineyards; in fact, it's pretty tricky to find 'foreign' wines apart from in large supermarkets. The choice of national wine is extensive and excellent, so you're sure to find something you enjoy, and alongside the usual options of red and white, you will also find vinho verde or green wine. Vinho verde is a popular daytime wine as it is younger, lower in alcohol and pleasantly light and effervescent.

Popular soft drinks are Sumol, a fizzy fruity soft drink that comes in a myriad of flavours including laranja (orange), ananás (pineapple) and maracujá (passionfruit). You will also see Guaraná served in most places; this is an import from Brazil, which is sweet and fizzy.

36. BACALHAU

Bacalhau is salt cod and is truly beloved in Portugal. In markets and grocers all over Portugal you will see cod that has been heavily salted then dried to preserve it. I comes in large rock solid sides and is designed to withstand the hottest Lisbon summer with no refrigeration required.

Before you cook the bacalhau, you need to rehydrate the dried fish by soaking it in water for about three days, changing the water every evening, then shred or slice it to use in recipes. People say that there are 365 ways to cook salt cod - one for each day of the year and you are likely to see several varieties on menus all over town.

37. TRY TRADITIONAL SOUR CHERRY LIQUEUR

Trying ginjinha whilst you're in Lisbon is a must. This potent liqueur is made from sour morello cherries soaked in a spirit called aguardente. The mixture is then sweetened with sugar and further favoured spices such as cinnamon.

Most bars serve it in a small shot glass, or in a dark chocolate cup which you can then munch on. A glass of ginjinha in Lisbon usually costs around €1 to €1.50. You can have your shot with or without the soaked cherries, locals usually go for keeping the cherry in the liquor but they are very sour when you bite into them and certainly pack an alcoholic punch.

Try one of the traditional old shops for a shot of ginjinha, A Ginjinha Espinheira is open all day every day until late into the evening and is easy to find just off Rossio Square, or Ginjinha Sem Rival which is close by.

38. VHILS STREET ART

Alexandre Farto aka Vhils was born in 1987 in Portugal and grew up just outside Lisbon. He returned to Portugal after studying at studied at the University of the Arts in London, Central Saint Martins, and Byam Shaw Fine Art Skills and Practices. Having grown up in an interesting period of political and social change in post-revolution his artistry was impacted by the changes he saw happening in Portugal. Vhils caught the publics' eye when one of his carved portraits was shown alongside street artist Banksy's work in London in 2008.

One of Vhils most iconic forms of art is the relief portrait chiseled into plaster and brick walls. He is also known for using etching acid, bleach, pneumatic drills, and other technical processes to reveal a wall's layers and create striking images. You can find 2 of his relief portraits on Rua Cais de Alcântara and on Avenida da India in Lisbon.

39. TRAIN ALONG THE LINHA

If the city gets too hot and crowded and you may need to escape to the seaside for the day. The good news is that Lisbon is poised just up the Tejo river from the beaches lining the Atlantic coast of Portugal. Cascais is a beautiful fishing village which became famous as a weekend haunt of the Portuguese royal family in the 1870s and has remained a sought after seaside retreat for Lisboetas today.

It couldn't be easier to catch the train out along the coastline from Lisbon, out to the seaside town of Cascais. From Cais do Sodre station you can hop on a train and be exploring along the coast in no time at all. The journey along the coast takes around 40 minutes and gives you a good sense of the geography of the area.

40. CASCAIS OLD TOWN AND MUSEUM DISTRICT

The Old Town is the most charming place to wander around, turn your back on the beach and head into the maze of streets and walkways between the square and Nossa Senhora de Assunção church. The main square is paved with the typical black and white Portuguese cobbles and ringed with bars and restaurants.

To find the secret places, away from all the tourists, head up the stairs next to Boulangerie Paul and get lost for a while. You'll stumble upon houses with beautiful tiled facades, secret gardens and the Gil Vincente theatre which was constructed in 1869. Enjoy strolling past the coloured shop fronts and homes and in the summer, enjoy the shade of the winding streets and alleyways.

Come out of the old town onto the small green area opposite the Museo del Mar and the Casa Paula Rego, and you'll be in the Museum District of Cascais.

Head around the corner towards the sea to the 15th-century fort that stands over the picturesque harbour. Go into the Cidadela de Cascais, which holds the bijou art district, a display of sculptures in the whitewashed square and a series of galleries where artists create and display their work.

The Centro Cultural de Cascais, a former convent, near the fort holds a series of temporary displays and has an interior which is well worth looking around on your way to the nearby museums.

The building which houses the Museo del Mar was constructed in 1859 on the instructions of Principe Carlos. The stories of the maritime history of the region and of Cascais itself are a fascinating insight into local history. Next door the pink conical roofs of the Casa Paula Rego are a local landmark. Celebrated Portuguese artist displays her work in this beautiful space, and there are often additional exhibitions to enjoy.

41. MARECHAL CARMONA PARK

This is a great park tucked away between the old town in Cascais and the seafront. As you walk into the park, you'll see the sweet little ornamental lake with bridges overlooking the duck houses, and turtles basking on the rocks. Head further into the park, past the children's play area, and you'll find the original sculptures that line the paths around the open green space.

If you come to the park on a Saturday, then you'll find an organic produce and handicraft market set up on the green. There is a small charity cafe where you'll see some of the park's resident hens and their chicks wandering around under the tables pecking at crumbs. Keep an eye out for the peacocks that call the park home, and they can surprise you with their loud shrieks!

42. MUSEU CONDES DE CASTRO GUIMARAES

✓

The park also houses the Museu Condes de Castro Guimarães, which is housed in a beautiful historic villa also known as the Tower of São Sebastião. The fairytale mansion was built in a medieval romantic style with elaborate interiors which are worth looking around. The chapel and elaborate azulejo tiles lion fountain beside the entrance is, believe it or not, a top place to play online game Pokemon Go!

Walked

43. BIKE ALONG THE RED PATH TO GUINCHO BEACH

✓

From Marechal Carmona park it's an easy walk along the coastal red path past the marina to Casa De Guia a walled esplanade with several bars and restaurants. At Casa de Guia you can stop for a drink and catch your breath overlooking the fabulous coastline after refreshments head to the MobiCascais kiosk provided by the town council and rent a bike or electric scooter.

Pedal power is the best way to get out to the beautiful Atlantic beaches of Guincho, and all you have to do is follow the red path and keep the sea to your left! Guincho is famed for its long stretch of golden sands and the top class waves popular with surfers. If you fancy surf lessons, head up to one of the surf schools, or if you'd prefer to relax with a drink, then there are two great beach bars.

44. BOCA DO INFERNO

On the way out of town towards Guincho to the west, stop off at Boca do Inferno or Mouth of Hell, this is a rocky promontory which has been eroded over the years to create a sea cave and archway through which the waves crash on a windy day. There are viewing points down on the rocks and a boardwalk to wander along to take in the ocean view.

If the sea is calm when you visit you might not see the full drama of the waves but sit here on the rocks at sunset and watch the sun drop into the Atlantic, and you'll feel your stresses melt away.

45. CASCAIS BEACHES

The beaches in Cascais are worth a visit while you are in town, Praia da Ribeira, known by locals as Fisherman's beach, is the beach opposite the main square. It is busy year-round with swimmers and teenagers using the permanent volleyball nets and is named for the small fishing fleet which still moors just offshore.

Praia da Rainha is so named as it was the private beach that Queen Amelia used when she holidayed in Cascais in the 19th century, and you can see why. It is a tucked-away cove with azure water, backed with rocky outcrops down a steep stairway from the main town, but because it's so picturesque and compact it gets busy quickly.

Slightly further along the promenade towards Estoril are the main beaches of Praia da Conceição and Praia da Duquesa which are linked to form a perfect stretch of sand with access to restaurants, sunbeds, and calm, clean waters. This is a great place to sunbathe in comfort before heading back to Lisbon on the train.

46. SINTRA UNESCO WORLD HERITAGE SITE

Sintra is a great day out within easy reach of Lisbon, you can get the train from Santa Apolonia station, and the journey will take you an hour giving you plenty of time to explore. If you hike and take the tram, you will avoid much of the tourist traffic that clogs the roads.

There is no denying it, Sintra is busy all year round, it is a UNESCO world heritage site, and the old part of town is a hub of activity with good reason. There are so many beautiful things to look at you don't know where to start. You can visit any number of fabulous palaces, castles and lookout points all within a stone's throw of each other. How would you like to do it entirely alone? When the roads up the hill to Palacio da Pena have been choc a block with tour buses and tuk-tuks, I have done these walks and not encountered a soul, even in the height of summer.

Enjoy a little peace and quiet and really take the time to soak up the atmosphere of the place chosen as a royal retreat since …. Hike up the shady forest path from Seteais Palace (38.795754110989506,-9.399141321856404) to the Castelo dos Mouros (38.79256005980313,-9.389362335205078) via the Pena Palace and back into town (38.78760942870899,-9.390649795532226) for a 1.5hr walk on the wild side in Sintra.

The Seteais Trail needs you to be fit and in good shape for walking as part of the route is pretty steep, and the footpath can be a little rugged. It follows a hiking trail along a hillside road that winds up to the palaces above the historic centre of Sintra, then takes off on a woodland track. Take a water bottle and maybe put one a pastry in your backpack and plan to take a breather on your way through the trees to look over the fantastic view.

An alternative walk for those who prefer something a little more comfortable and more relaxed is the Santa Maria Trail which starts from the Casa Info Parques de Sintra (38.473886,- 9.230098) close to the historic centre. The walk is graded 'easy,' and it will take around an hour to walk the mainly paved paths past the Moorish Castle and up to the grounds of Pena Palace.

Whichever trail you take up to Pena Palace an excellent way to descend is the Lapa Trail. This trail leads from the main entrance of the grounds of Pena Palace back down into town. It is a mainly forested path and is easy, although it does have a few short steep downhill sloping areas.

It is always wise to check with the Sintra Parks Service to pick up a map, ensure that the trails are open and let them know that you're heading into the woods.

47. TRADITIONAL SINTRA TREATS

The travesseiros pastries, puff pastry filled with almond custard that Sintra is famous for have been baked daily at the landmark Piriquita bakery tucked away in the old part of town since 1862.

48. SINTRA

Quinta da Regaleira is a fantastic house and grounds which looks as if has come straight out of a Brothers Grimm fairytale. Built initially for eccentric millionaire and Brazilian businessman Antonio Caralho Monteiro the house and gardens were designed and built to his specifications and catered to his interests in alchemy, Freemasonry, the Knights Templar, and Christian mythology.

In the extensive forested gardens, you will find riddles and surprises tucked away around every turn of the 10 acres. You'll stumble across fairy doors, grottos, towers to climb and underground tunnels to get lost in. See if you can find the tunnel hidden behind an old fountain and find the tower with the 6 point star candle chandelier.

This UNESCO world heritage site lies around 20 on foot out of town (or hop on a bus from the station), and if you come early, you have a chance of wandering around the neo-gothic house and grounds undisturbed. The most photographed site in the gardens are the initiation wells, so-called because of a supposed connection to the rites of the Knights Templar and Freemasons. The wells are 27 metres deep, and you can descend the entire way via a long spiral staircase divided into nine levels which are said to mirror the nine circles of Hell of Dante's Inferno. At the bottom, you will find not only a fascinating Rosicrucian mosaic but also a secret tunnel that leads to a myriad of underground passageways that ramble beneath the gardens.

Although parts of the house itself are open to the public to explore, it is the grounds that are the real attraction of the Quinta, and you will want to take your time exploring them.

49. TRAM TRIP TO APPLE BEACH

The trams that connect Sintra to Praia das Macas or Apple Beach beach 13km beneath are classic vehicles from the 1930s and take around 40 minutes to wend their way down to Praia das Maçãs. There might be a line outside the tram stop, but the slow, bumpy journey down to the coast is well worth the wait. The landscape changes as you descend the hills to the coast, and it's a fun way to appreciate the countryside. You will bump along through the trees and at the side of country roads in the red Bell tram, or Electrico as it is known in Portuguese and feel yourself unwinding.

Praia das Maçãs is a bustling little cove with gentle waves and lots of rock pools to explore at low tide. You can take a walk along the clifftop or enjoy a meal at one of the restaurants that line the promenade; the fish is usually excellent and very fresh. If you visit in the summer, you'll see signs hanging outside eateries advising that 'ha sardinhas,' sardines are available.

50. NOT JUST A SUMMER DESTINATION

Did you know that Lisbon is the sunniest capital in Europe? Well, it is, average temperatures for the coldest month of January show a low of 8c and a high of 15c and as someone who was in a T-shirt on the beach outside Lisbon on Christmas Day 2018, I can confirm that the winter sun is warm. Even if it feels chilly, the sun is often out, any way you don't want it too warm, or you'll melt walking up all the hills in the historic Alfama and Bairro Alto districts.

Whether you prefer to wander around and discover the secrets tucked around corners in winding roads yourself or join a walking tour of the city, you're best placed to get to know Lisbon on foot. August temperatures are regularly in the 30c range and combined with crowds; it's easy to become exhausted and not enjoy your break.

Lisbon is a living city; it's not somewhere that is only open in the summer, Lisboetas like to work hard then get out in the evening to enjoy themselves all year round. Even in the winter, you can find people dining or having a drink outside, bring a jacket, or tuck a scarf in your bag. Sure, you'll replace ice cream with a coffee or a hot chocolate in the morning, but the rooftop bars will still be going strong in the evening. Enjoy cocktails at one of the epic rooftop bars with river views and great DJs or find a fado hideaway in the older part of town. The weather definitely doesn't stop play here.

PACKING AND PLANNING TIPS

A Week before Leaving

- Arrange for someone to take care of pets and water plants.

- Email and Print important Documents.

- Get Visa and vaccines if needed.

- Check for travel warnings.

- Stop mail and newspaper.

- Notify Credit Card companies where you are going.

- Passports and photo identification is up to date.

- Pay bills.

- Copy important items and download travel Apps.

- Start collecting small bills for tips.

- Have post office hold mail while you are away.

- Check weather for the week.

- Car inspected, oil is changed, and tires have the correct pressure.

- Check airline luggage restrictions.

- Download Apps needed for your trip.

Right Before Leaving

- Contact bank and credit cards to tell them your location.

- Clean out refrigerator.

- Empty garbage cans.

- Lock windows.

- Make sure you have the proper identification with you.

- Bring cash for tips.

- Remember travel documents.

- Lock door behind you.

- Remember wallet.

- Unplug items in house and pack chargers.

- Change your thermostat settings.

- Charge electronics, and prepare camera memory cards.

READ OTHER
GREATER THAN A TOURIST
BOOKS

Greater Than a Tourist- Geneva Switzerland: 50 Travel Tips from a Local by Amalia Kartika

Greater Than a Tourist- St. Croix US Birgin Islands USA: 50 Travel Tips from a Local by Tracy Birdsall

Greater Than a Tourist- San Juan Puerto Rico: 50 Travel Tips from a Local by Melissa Tait

Greater Than a Tourist – Lake George Area New York USA: 50 Travel Tips from a Local by Janine Hirschklau

Greater Than a Tourist – Monterey California United States: 50 Travel Tips from a Local by Katie Begley

Greater Than a Tourist – Chanai Crete Greece: 50 Travel Tips from a Local by Dimitra Papagrigoraki

Greater Than a Tourist – The Garden Route Western Cape Province South Africa: 50 Travel Tips from a Local by Li-Anne McGregor van Aardt

Greater Than a Tourist – Sevilla Andalusia Spain: 50 Travel Tips from a Local by Gabi Gazon

Children's Book: *Charlie the Cavalier Travels the World* by Lisa Rusczyk

> TOURIST

Follow us on Instagram for beautiful travel images:
http://Instagram.com/GreaterThanATourist

Follow *Greater Than a Tourist* on Amazon.

> TOURIST

At *Greater Than a Tourist*, we love to share travel tips with you. How did we do? What guidance do you have for how we can give you better advice for your next trip? Please send your feedback to GreaterThanaTourist@gmail.com as we continue to improve the series. We appreciate your constructive feedback. Thank you.

METRIC CONVERSIONS

TEMPERATURE

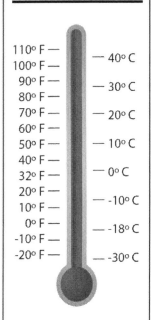

110° F — — 40° C
100° F —
90° F — — 30° C
80° F —
70° F — — 20° C
60° F —
50° F — — 10° C
40° F —
32° F — — 0° C
20° F —
10° F — — -10° C
0° F — — -18° C
-10° F —
-20° F — — -30° C

To convert F to C:

Subtract 32, and then multiply by 5/9 or .5555.

To Convert C to F:

Multiply by 1.8
and then add 32.

32F = 0C

LIQUID VOLUME

To Convert:................Multiply by
U.S. Gallons to Liters................ 3.8
U.S. Liters to Gallons 26
Imperial Gallons to U.S. Gallons 1.2
Imperial Gallons to Liters....... 4.55
Liters to Imperial Gallons 22
1 Liter = .26 U.S. Gallon
1 U.S. Gallon = 3.8 Liters

DISTANCE

To convert ....Multiply by
Inches to Centimeters 2.54
Centimeters to Inches 39
Feet to Meters...................... .3
Meters to Feet 3.28
Yards to Meters 91
Meters to Yards 1.09
Miles to Kilometers 1.61
Kilometers to Miles............ .62
1 Mile = 1.6 km
1 km = .62 Miles

WEIGHT

1 Ounce = .28 Grams
1 Pound = .4555 Kilograms
1 Gram = .04 Ounce
1 Kilogram = 2.2 Pounds

TRAVEL QUESTIONS

- Do you bring presents home to family or friends after a vacation?

- Do you get motion sick?

- Do you have a favorite billboard?

- Do you know what to do if there is a flat tire?

- Do you like a sun roof open?

- Do you like to eat in the car?

- Do you like to wear sun glasses in the car?

- Do you like toppings on your ice cream?

- Do you use public bathrooms?

- Did you bring your cell phone and does it have power?

- Do you have a form of identification with you?

- Have you ever been pulled over by a cop?

- Have you ever given money to a stranger on a road trip?

- Have you ever taken a road trip with animals?

- Have you ever went on a vacation alone?

- Have you ever run out of gas?

- If you could move to any place in the world, where would it be?

- If you could travel anywhere in the world, where would you travel?

- If you could travel in any vehicle, which one would it be?

- If you had three things to wish for from a magic genie, what would they be?

- If you have a driver's license, how many times did it take you to pass the test?

- What are you the most afraid of on vacation?

- What do you want to get away from the most when you are on vacation?

- What foods smells bad to you?

- What item do you bring on ever trip with you away from home?

- What makes you sleepy?

- What song would you love to hear on the radio when you're cruising on the highway?

- What travel job would you want the least?

- What will you miss most while you are away from home?

- What is something you always wanted to try?

- What is the best road side attraction that you ever saw?

- What is the farthest distance you ever biked?

- What is the farthest distance you ever walked?

- What is the weirdest thing you needed to buy while on vacation?

- What is your favorite candy?

- What is your favorite color car?

- What is your favorite family vacation?

- What is your favorite food?

- What is your favorite gas station drink or food?

- What is your favorite license plate design?

- What is your favorite restaurant?

- What is your favorite smell?

- What is your favorite song?

- What is your favorite sound that nature makes?

- What is your favorite thing to bring home from a vacation?

- What is your favorite vacation with friends?

- What is your favorite way to relax?

- Where is the farthest place you ever traveled in a car?

- Where is the farthest place you ever went North, South, East and West?

- Where is your favorite place in the world?

- Who is your favorite singer?

- Who taught you how to drive?

- Who will you miss the most while you are away?

- Who if the first person you will contact when you get to your destination?

- Who brought you on your first vacation?

- Who likes to travel the most in your life?

- Would you rather be hot or cold?

- Would you rather drive above, below, or at the speed limited?

- Would you rather drive on a highway or a back road?

- Would you rather go on a train or a boat?

- Would you rather go to the beach or the woods?

TRAVEL BUCKET LIST

1.

2.

3.

4.

5.

6.

7.

8.

9.

10.

NOTES

Printed in Great Britain
by Amazon